Contents

Introduction 2

Getting Started 3

Fabric for Framing Your Artwork:
Picking just the right fabric for your project 3

Choosing Your Artwork:
Cross-stitch, printed pictures, machine embroidery, handwork 4

Getting to Work 7

Step-by-Step Directions:
The basics of construction 7

Adding the Frame:
Easy instructions for mitering corners *10*

Quilting Your Framed Artwork:
Easy quilting with your walking foot—in the ditches, real or fake 15

Finishing Up

Hanging Corners 17

Binding 18

Gallery of Framed Artwork 25

About the Author & Acknowledgments 31

Introduction

This technique is fun, fast, and easy. As a beginner, you will learn all basic quilting techniques. As an experienced quilter, you will have the opportunity to get as creative as you would like.

When you go into someone's home, usually you'll see beautiful pictures on the walls of their families, especially grandchildren, or a beautiful cross-stitch work that has taken hours and hours of effort. Maybe it's Christmas and they have some cute seasonal pictures. My technique is a new way to use striped fabrics to frame your own artwork and place it on the wall for your company to admire.

My fabric-framing technique can be used to create a special gift for the person who appreciates your quilting talent. It could be a picture of your family, hand or machine embroidery, or a piece of needlework. Feel free to add some unique quilting, embellishing, or painting ideas of your own.

GETTING STARTED

Fabric for Framing Your Artwork: *Picking just the right fabric for your project*

First of all, the "Hunt for the Fabric" is part of the fun. When making that weekly trip to your favorite fabric store, or finding a new shop along your travels, keep an eye out for fun and unusual striped fabrics.

I like to call this collection of striped and border fabrics my "frame fabrics."

Getting Started

Choosing Your Artwork:
Cross-stitch, printed pictures, machine embroidery, handwork

The next step after building a stash of wonderful striped fabrics is to choose something you want to frame. This is where the family pictures, cross-stitch embroideries, handwork, etc., come in.

Here is a selection of handmade cross-stitch pieces, printed family pictures, and machine embroidery.

Getting Started

Once you have chosen your artwork, the fun comes in choosing what part of the frame fabric you want to use. You can choose several stripes of one fabric, or choose from two or three different frame fabrics. Be creative.

GETTING STARTED

Fig. 1

All three centers in these pieces are cut from the same fabric!

The frames are also all from a single piece of fabric. I chose an oriental panel and a striped coordinating fabric. From these I cut different centerpieces and chose coordinating stripes for the frames (Fig. 1).

Basic Supplies:
What you need for your project

SUPPLIES LIST

You don't need any special supplies to frame your artwork other than what you'd need for any quilting project.

- Artwork to be framed: embroidery, patchwork, cross-stitch, photographs printed on fabric, etc.
- Frame/striped fabric for the frame and binding—at least ¾ of a yard; a full yard is better
- Rotary cutter, rotary-cutting mat, and ruler
- Scissors
- Grey or beige thread for piecing
- Decorative thread for quilting
- 100 percent cotton batting
- Backing
- Wooden dowel for hanging

Getting to Work

Step-by-Step Instructions:
The basics of construction

For demonstrating my framing technique, I chose to print a picture of my grandson and his bride on June Tailor® Sew-In Computer Printer Fabric™ using my printer (Fig. 2). There are many types of printable fabrics available; use your favorite. They all work well with this technique.

After printing your image, allow it to dry. Remove the paper from the back and press with a dry iron to heat set.

Trim your artwork to the desired size.

SPECIAL TIP!

Be sure to use a dry iron on the printed pictures. If your iron leaks, the picture will blur.

Fig. 2

Getting to Work

For the best results, audition different fabrics to choose one or more frame fabrics that enhance your artwork.

Fig. 3

Fig. 4

Fig. 5

Fig. 6

I chose the first blue stripe because it highlighted the photograph; the others made it look dull and I thought the fourth one (Fig. 6) was too light.

Getting to Work

Once you have chosen your frame fabric, select which stripes you want to use from it. Double-check that your chosen stripes don't have a two-way pattern. In this example, the fans face in opposite directions (Fig. 7).

Using these strips would result in non-matching frames.

Special Tip!

Double check that your fabric does not have a two-way pattern in it, such as the fans that go two ways in this fabric.

Frame Cutting Tip!

When you cut your frames, add ¼" seam allowances on both sides of your chosen frame fabric. Be sure to cut as accurately as possible.

Fig. 7

Cut four identical frames. The length of each should equal the side of the artwork plus two times the width of the frame strips. You need this additional length for mitering the corners. Be as accurate as possible—you will be much happier if they are all straight.

You can see here how the frame strips have been cut longer than the size of the artwork itself (Fig. 8).

Fig. 8

Adding the Frame: *Easy instructions for mitering corners*

Mark a ¼" seam allowance at the four corners on the back side of your artwork (Fig. 9).

Matching the centers of your frames with the center of the sides (Fig. 10), sew the four frames to the artwork, starting and stopping exactly ¼" from the corners (Fig. 11). Backstitch for security (Fig. 12).

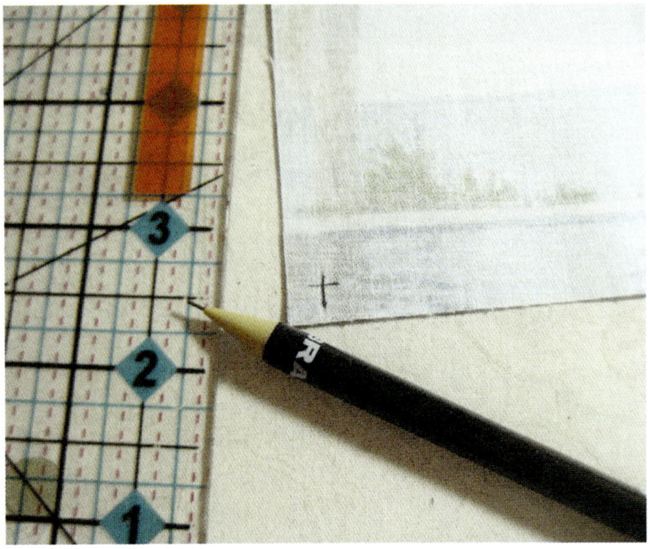

Fig. 9

Fig. 10

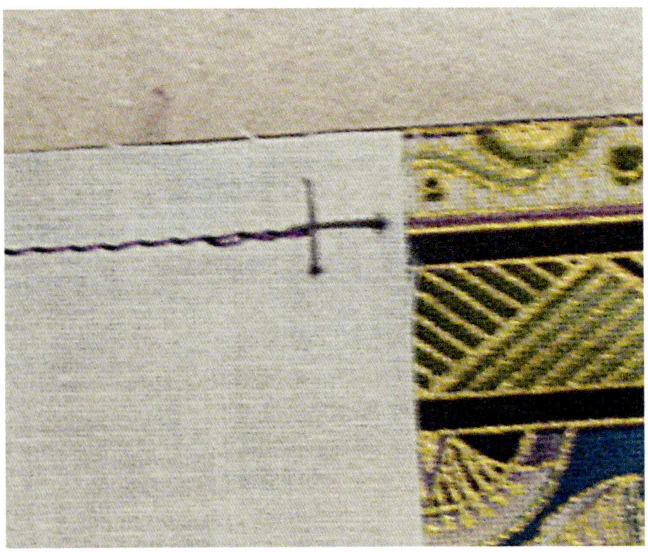

Fig. 11

Fig. 12

Getting to Work

Fold the artwork on the diagonal, wrong sides together, aligning the edges of the extra frame fabric that extends beyond the artwork. Pin in place (Fig. 13).

Lay your artwork flat, face down, and mark a 45-degree sewing line on the frame fabric (Fig. 14). To assure accuracy, place a ruler along horizontal design elements of the fabric prints to find the 45-degree angle (Fig. 15).

Fig. 13

Fig. 14

Fig. 15

Fig. 16

Stick pins into the design lines along the drawn sewing line, making sure the design matches on both sides. Carefully pin in place (Fig. 16).

Switch to an open-toe foot so you can see exactly where to sew. Sew along the drawn line from the ¼" point on the artwork toward the outside corner (Fig. 17).

Double check that the design matches on the front of your mitered corner. Now is the time to fix any problems. Then trim the excess fabric to a ¼" seam allowance (Fig 18). Press the mitered seam open and the artwork seams toward the frame (Fig. 19).

Fig. 17

Fig. 18

Fig. 19

Getting to Work

Fig. 20

The front of your mitered corners should lie flat and match perfectly (Fig. 20).

SPECIAL TIP!

When pressing open your mitered seam the artwork seams should be pressed toward the frame to lie nice and flat.

Repeat on the remaining three corners. Here is how both the back (Fig. 21) and front (Fig. 22) look after sewing all four corners.

Fig. 21

Fig. 22

Getting to Work

Cut your batting and backing slightly larger than the frame and layer for quilting (Fig. 23). I prefer 100 percent cotton and use a spray-basting adhesive to hold the layers together.

Fig. 23

Quilting Your Framed Artwork:
Easy quilting with your walking foot – in the ditches, real or fake

Quilting can be a simple straight stitch in the ditch. A "real" ditch is the low side of a seam, either where you joined the frame to the artwork or along the seams if you used multiple fabrics to create your frames (Fig. 24).

A "fake" ditch is stitching along one of your frame fabric design lines, making it look like a real seam line (Fig. 25).

Use a walking foot when quilting to keep your top, batting, and backing from slipping. Most sewing machines have an attachable walking foot, some machines have built in walking feet. If you are free-motion quilting, use an open-toe free-motion or darning foot.

Fig. 24

Fig. 25

Finishing Up

Fig. 26

After quilting your project, trim the outside edges, and use some of the frame fabric to bind your project (Fig. 26).

Finishing Up

Fig. 27

Fig. 28

Hanging Corners:

Cut two squares of backing or frame fabric. The size depends on the size of your framed artwork, although I find that 6" x 6" is a good size for most pieces.

Fold the squares in half on the diagonal, wrong sides together, and press, forming two triangles (Fig. 27).

Pin the triangles on the back top corners of your quilted artwork, aligning the raw edges with the raw edges of your quilt (Fig. 28).

These will be sewn in place as you sew on the binding.

Finishing Up

Binding:

Carefully cut as many 2½" strips from the frame fabric as needed to go around your quilted piece, plus at least 10" for the extra fabric needed for the seams and to turn the corners. You may need more if you want to match the pattern at the seams precisely.

Join the strips, carefully matching the design in the fabrics. I prefer using a 45-degree angle seam, which cuts down the bulk at the seams (Figs. 29–33).

Fig. 29

Fig. 30

Fig. 31

Fig. 32

Fig. 33

Finishing Up

Fig. 34

You may find it easier to match the design with a straight seam (Figs. 34 and 35).

Fold the binding strip in half lengthwise, wrong sides together, and press.

Place the folded binding at the center of one edge of the quilted artwork and start sewing with a ¼" seam allowance several inches from the center, leaving a beginning tail (Fig. 36).

Fig. 35

Fig. 36

FINISHING UP

Sew within ¼" of the corner (Fig. 37). Pull the piece out of the machine and fold the binding back away from the quilt at a 45-degree angle (Fig. 38).

Fold the binding back down, aligning the fold with the edge of the side just sewn and the raw edges with the next side of the quilt (Fig. 39). Sew to the next corner with a ¼" seam. Continue around the quilt completing all four corners the same way.

Fig. 37

Fig. 38

Fig. 39

Fig. 40

Sew to within about 8" of where you began sewing the binding. To connect the beginning and ending tails, fold both tails back leaving a small space between them. This small space allows for the binding to fit perfectly when completed (Fig. 40).

Cut the left tail on the fold line (Fig. 41). Using the cut-off piece as a guide, open it up, lay it on top of the right side of the binding and trim the right binding off this much beyond the fold (Fig. 42). (This measurement should be beyond the fold by the width of the unfolded binding strip—in this case, 2½".)

Fig. 41

Fig. 42

Finishing Up

Fig. 43

Fig. 44

Fold the left tail back at a 45-degree angle. This fold line will be your sewing line.

Take the right cut edge and pin to the top edge of the left side. Sew on the fold line, trim the seam allowance to ¼", and press open (Fig. 43).

Fold the binding into place and finish sewing the ¼" seam (Fig. 44).

Finishing Up

Fold the binding to the back side and hand stitch in place, covering up the seam line (Fig. 45). The four corners will automatically miter on the front and back (Fig. 46).

Fig. 45

Fig. 46

Alternatively, you can machine stitch the binding by folding it to the back, then machine stitch in the ditch from the front, making sure to catch the folded edge of the binding on the back (Fig. 47).

The hanging corners will be secured by the binding.

Fig. 47

Finishing Up

Slip a precut small dowel into the corners and hang your finished pieced on the wall.

Gallery of Framed Artwork

Gallery of Framed Artwork

USA
United States of America

Walking in a
Winter Wonderland

Gallery of Framed Artwork

Peony

Gallery of Framed Artwork

About the Author

Meet Sherry Fourez

Sherry Fourez has been a quilter and quilt teacher since 1987 after her husband, William, suggested she take a quilt class at a local church. It wasn't long before Sherry started teaching classes.

Sherry has been published in several magazines and in the AQS book Oh, Wow! The Miniature Quilts and Their Makers. She also has a miniature quilt in the collection of The National Quilt Museum in Paducah, Kentucky.

Sparkling Pineapple by Sherry Fourez

Acknowledgments

My special thanks go to my wonderful husband, William, for supporting me through all my crazy times, good and bad.

Thanks to all my quilting friends who encourage me and make me feel special every day.

I was lucky to have received several beautiful cross-stitch treasures from a friend after her passing. Marge Fillenworth did beautiful work. Please enjoy our combined work.

While I have made every effort to ensure that the directions in this book are clear and accurate, no warranty is given nor guaranteed for fabric choice, tools, human error, or personal skill.

More AQS Books

This is only a small selection of the books available from the American Quilter's Society. AQS books are known worldwide for timely topics, clear writing, beautiful color photos, and accurate illustrations and patterns. The following books are available from your local bookseller, quilt shop, or public library.

#1299

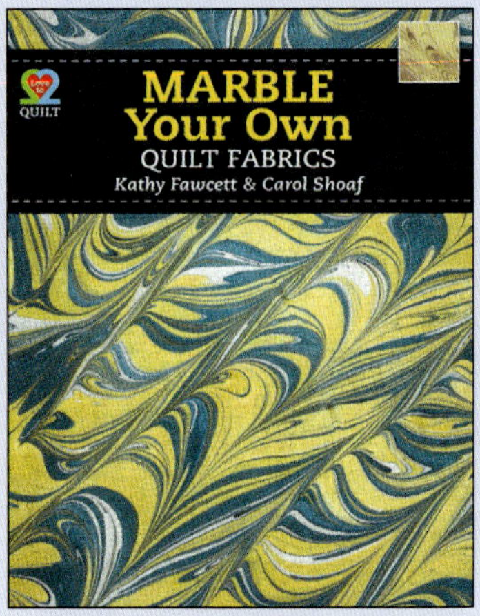

#1298

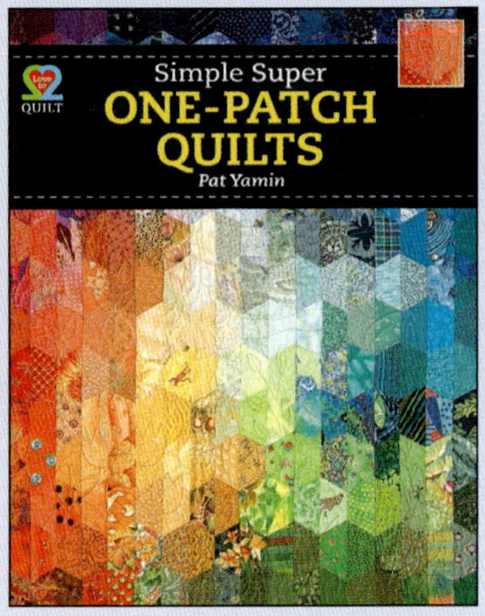

#1275

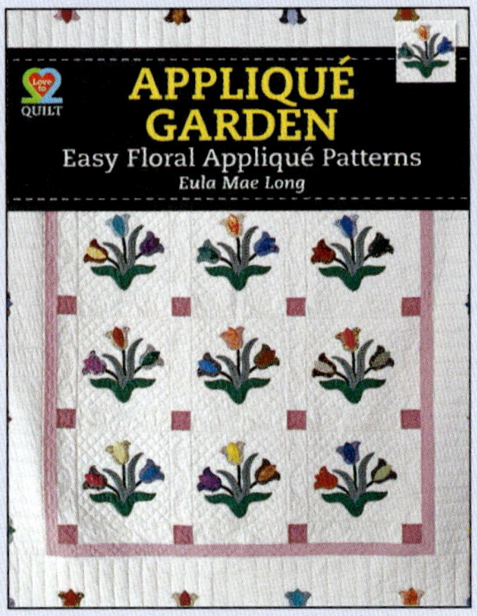

#1280

#1281

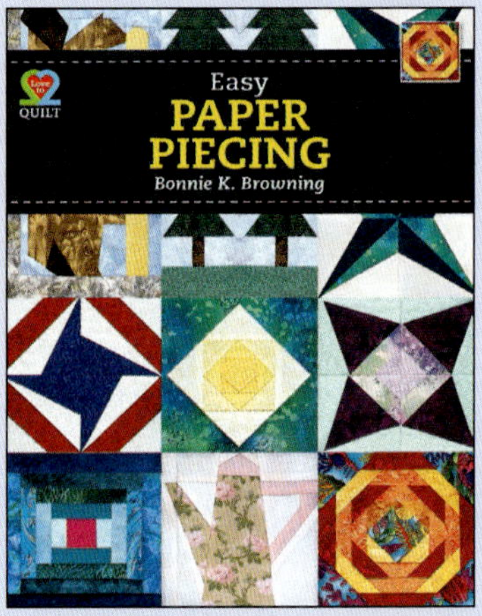

#1279

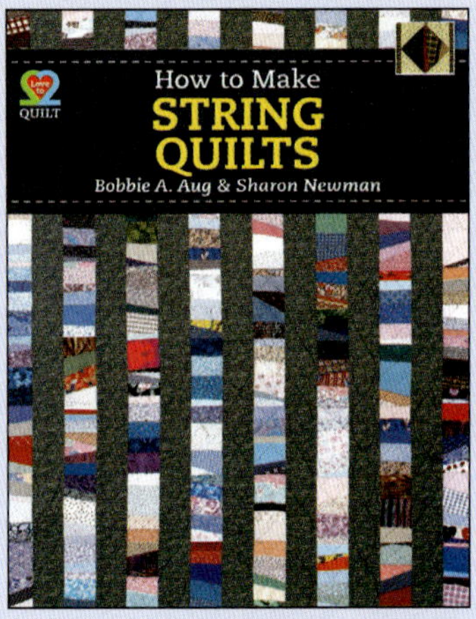

#1282

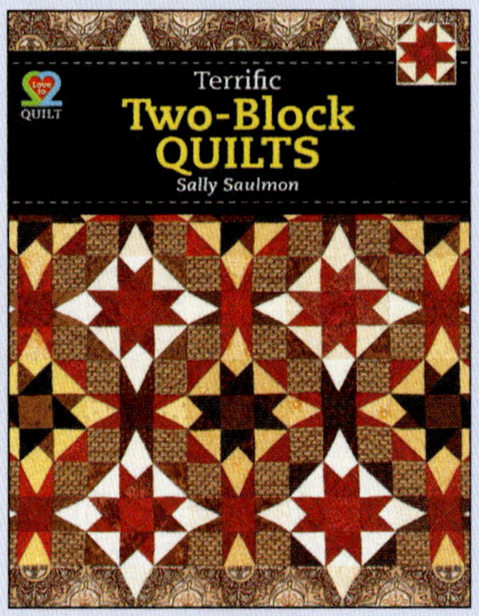

#1283

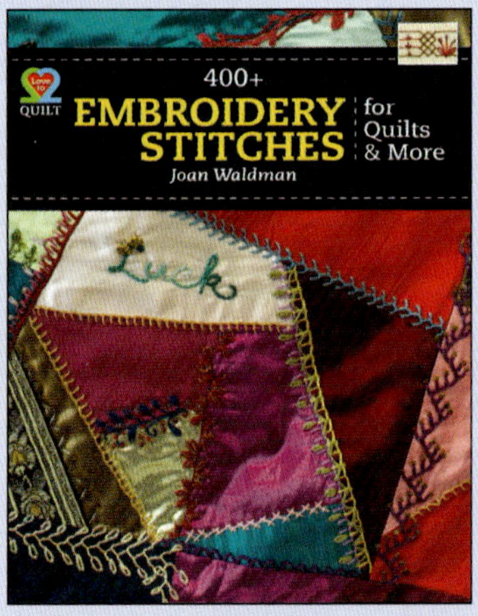

#1274

LOOK for these books nationally.
CALL or **VISIT** our website at

1-800-626-5420
www.AmericanQuilter.com